Let's rhyme!

Look at the pictures below and say what they are. Four of them have the same end sound. They all **rhyme**. Can you spot the one that does **not** rhyme? Draw a circle around it.

van

fan

pan

pin

man

Explain that words that sound the same at the end are words that rhyme. When your child has found the non-rhyming word see if they can think of a words that rhymes with it.

Build a word

Finger-trace each big letter as you say its sound.

Clever Cat   Annie Apple   Talking Tess

Touch the red dot under each letter as you say each sound.

c a t
. . .

Blend the first two sounds together. Then add the third sound.

ca t
→ .

Now say all three sounds together.

cat
→

Blend Remember to only whisper Clever Cat and Talking Tess's sounds. To blend 'cat' say the first two sounds together: 'ca...'. Say again and add **t** without a gap: 'cat'.

2

Rhyming words

Write the first letter. Say its sound. Blend the sounds to read each word.

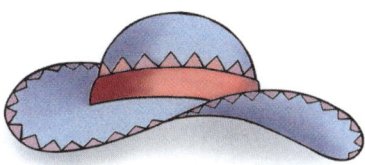

hat

mat

Say the rhyming words in the sentence below. Colour the picture.

Look at that fat cat in a hat on a mat!

Build a word

Bouncy Ben   **Eddy Elephant**   **Dippy Duck**

Touch the dots and finger-trace the arrows to blend the word.

b   e   d

be   d

bed

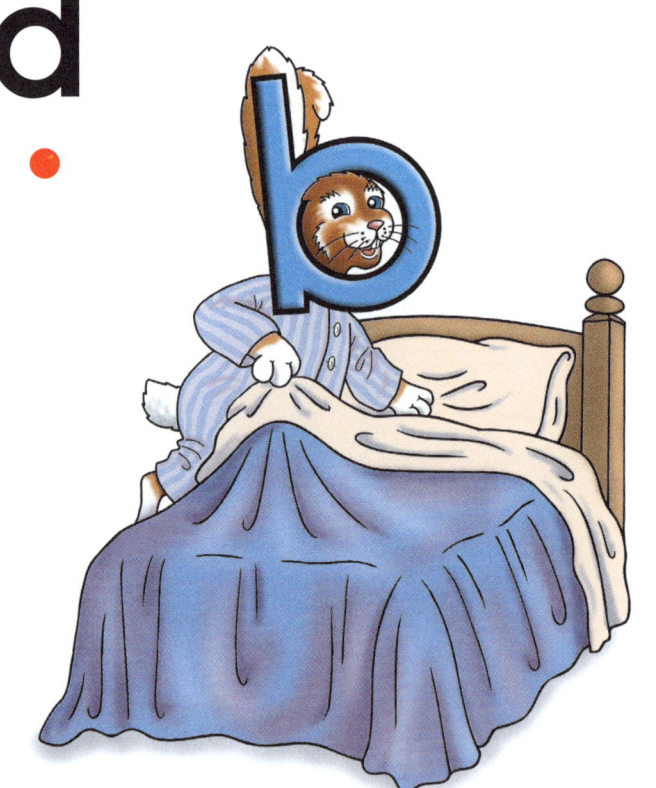

Blend Look at the top of the page. Say each Letterlander's sound together. To blend **'bed'** say the first two sounds together: **'be…'**. Say again and add **d** without a gap: **'bed'**.

Rhyming words

Write the first letter. Say its sound. Blend the sounds to read each word.

bed

Ted

Say the rhyming words in the sentence below. Colour the picture.

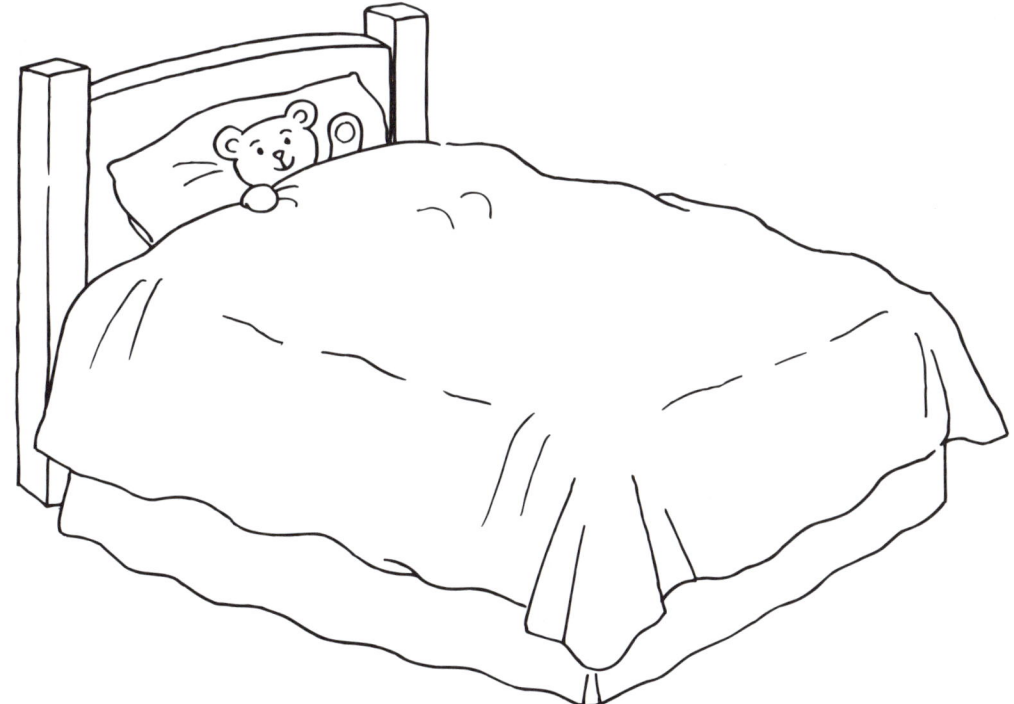

Ted is in a big, red bed!

Capitals: Explain that people's names always start with one uppercase letter. Write your child's name. What is the teddy bear's name? (Ted) Point to the red rhyming words together as you both say the sentence.

Build a word

Dippy Duck Impy Ink Golden Girl

Touch the dots and finger-trace the arrows to blend the word.

d i g

di g

dig

Blend  Look at the top of the page. Say each Letterlander's sound together. To blend '**dig**' say the first two sounds together: '**di…**'. Say again and add **g** without a gap: '**dig**'.

Rhyming words

Write the letter. Say its sound. Blend the word.

dig

wig

Say the rhyming words in the sentence below. Colour the picture.

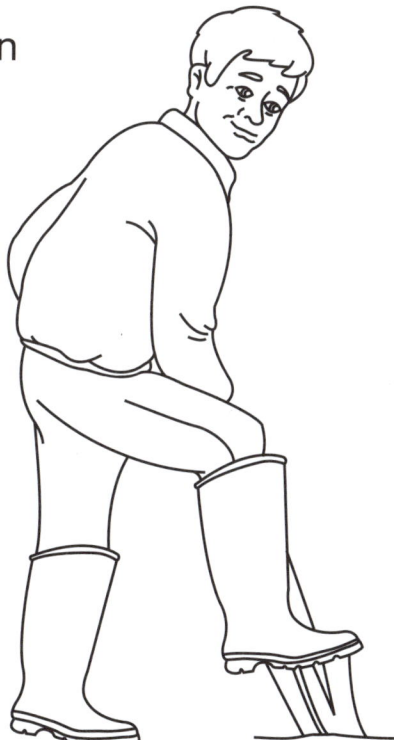

The big man in a wig likes to dig!

Listen — As you go over the blue words, encourage your child to listen to the way they sound alike at the end. Explain that this makes them into **rhyming** words. While colouring the picture, your child could say this rhyming sentence over and over again with you.

Build a word

Reading Direction

Dippy Duck   Oscar Orange   Golden Girl

Touch the dots and finger-trace the arrows to blend the word.

d   o   g

.   .   .

do   g

→   .

dog

→

Blend Look at the top of the page. Say each Letterlander's sound together. To blend '**dog**' say the first two sounds together: '**do...**'. Say again and add **g** without a gap: '**dog**'.

Rhyming words

Write the letter. Say its sound. Blend the word.

jog　　　log

Say the rhyming words in the sentence below. Colour the picture.

This dog likes to jog with a log!

Say the sentence together several times. Have some fun and make a game of saying the orange rhyming words louder than the rest of the sentence.

Build a word

Reading Direction

Bouncy Ben   Uppy Umbrella   Golden Girl

Touch the dots and finger-trace the arrows to blend the word.

Blend Look at the top of the page. Say each Letterlander's sound together. To blend 'bug' say the first two sounds together: 'bu...'. Say again and add **g** without a gap: 'bug'.

Rhyming words

Write the letter. Say its sound. Blend the word.

hug

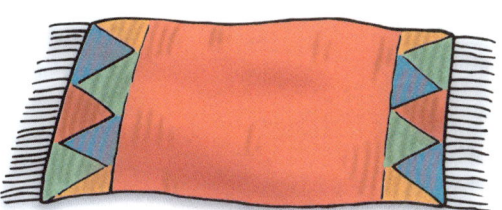

rug

Say the rhyming words in the sentence below. Colour the picture.

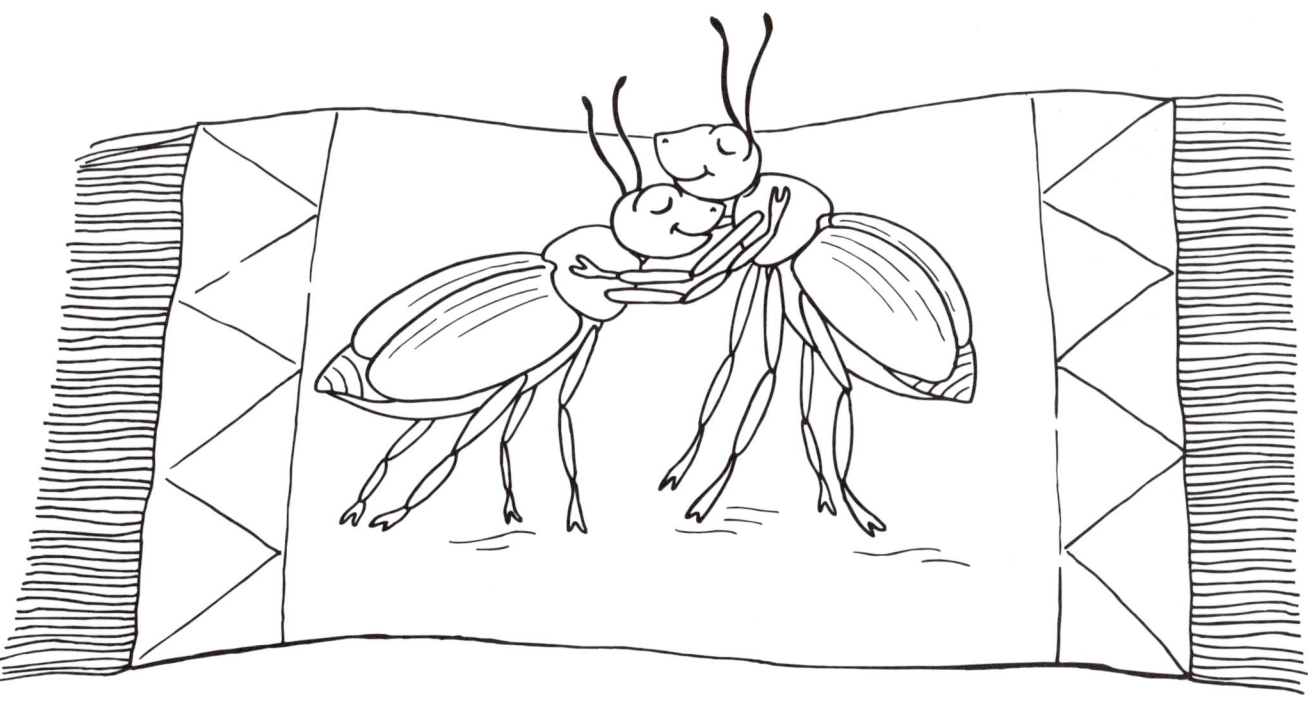

A big bug hug on a rug!

Rhyme — Follow up this activity by saying the phrase, 'Snug as a bug in a rug' together. Use it again tonight when you tuck your child into bed! And add, "That's a rhyme!"

Find the rhyming word

Look at the pictures below. Find the rhyming word and draw a circle around it.

map	tap	bee
hen	pen	bed
top	jelly	mop

Silly sentences

 Make up silly sentences using the rhyming words on each line. E.g. "There's a tap on that map". Make up as many as you can - the sillier the better!

Finish the rhyming pictures

Complete the pictures that rhyme. Cross out the ones that don't.

clock

sock

fox

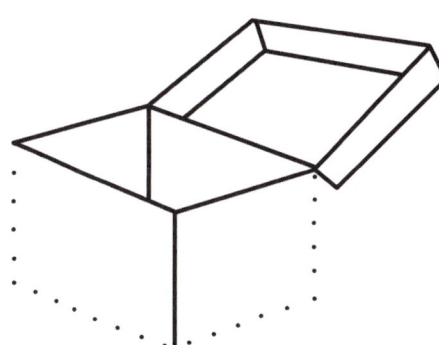
box

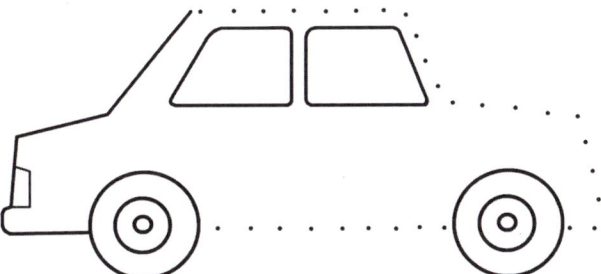
car

cat

Follow up this activity by asking your child to think of a rhyming word for the words that they have crossed out.

Match the rhyming words

Draw lines between the words that rhyme.

peg

fox

box

spoon

moon

egg

Explain to your child that a ryhme doesn't always **look** the same at the end, but it does always **sound** the same.

Match the rhyming words as before. Now, point to the Letterlander (above) that starts each word.

cake

hat

cup

snake

bat

pup

Rhyme — See if you child can think of a word the rhymes with each of the Letterlanders at the top of this page. E.g. **Ben - pen**; **Cat - rat**...

Odd one out

Cross out the two words that do not rhyme.

dog

bed

frog

ring

log

jog

Did your child spot the two non-rhyming words? Can they think of a word that rhymes with each of them?

Join the dots

Join the dots to make pictures of the rhyming words.

cat

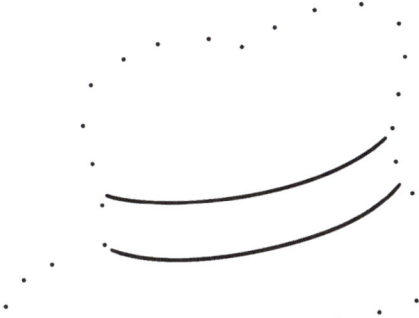
hat

truck

duck

car

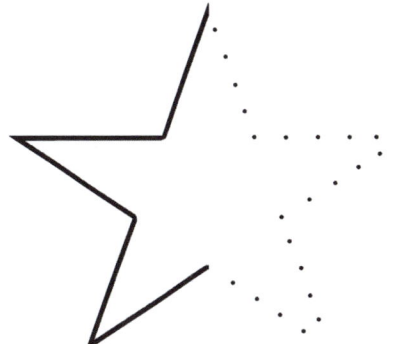
star

Pencil control — Joining the dots to complete the pictures encourages good pencil control - an essential element for successful letter formation.

Find the rhyming words

Find objects in the picture that rhyme with the word '**bug**'.

bug

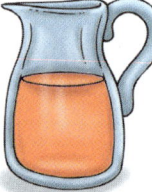
jug

mug

rug

slug

Now, find objects that rhyme with the word '**mat**'. Colour in both pictures.

Complete the words

Add Talking Tess's letter to finish these rhyming words.

ca __   ra __

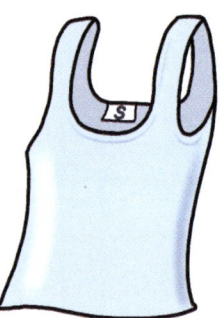

nes __   ves __

boa __   coa __

Tip Make sure your child uses the Letterland Sound Trick when making letter sounds. **Talking Tess** says 't...' not 'tuh' or 'tee'.

Complete the words

Add Noisy Nick's letter to finish these rhyming words.

he __

te __

moo __

spoo __

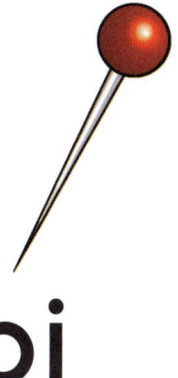

pi __

ti __

Tip — Make sure your child uses the Letterland Sound Trick when making letter sounds. **N**oisy **N**ick says '**nnn**...' not 'nuh' or 'en'.

Harry Hat Man's rhymes

Circle the pictures that rhyme with the last word in Harry Hat Man's name.

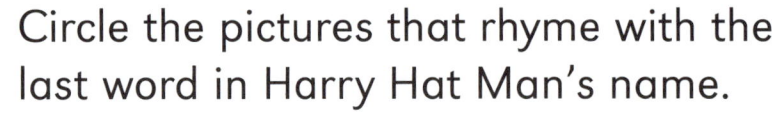
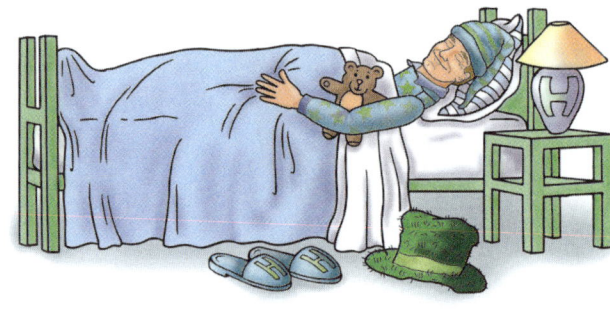

bed

pan

ball

van

fan

Have fun thinking up words that rhyme with the other words in Harry Hat Man's name. How many words can you both think of that rhyme with 'Harry' and 'Hat'?

Complete the rhyming words

Write in the first letter to complete the rhyming words. The Letterlanders (below) will help you.

 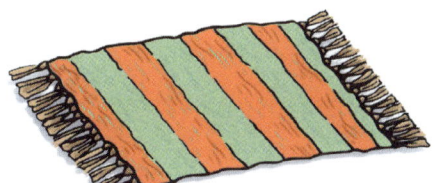 

__at   __at   __at

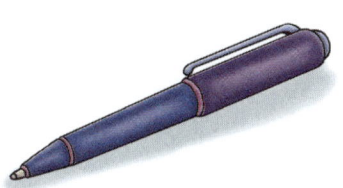  

__en   __en   __en

__op   __op   __op

Listen — Try to think of one more word that rhymes with each of these ending sounds.

Sammy's sentence rhymes

Read the rhymes below. Underline the rhyming words. Then draw a picture to go with each rhyme.

A cat sat on a mat.

I like to run in the sun.